REOPENING THE TRIAL
OF JESUS CHRIST

by

Dr. Wesley A. Swift

1970

Published by

NEW CHRISTIAN CRUSADE CHURCH
P.O. BOX 3247
HOLLYWOOD, CALIF. 90028

ISBN: 978-2-925369-64-6
Printed in the USA.

REOPENING THE TRIAL

OF JESUS CHRIST

The trial of Jesus Christ is a subject which is little understood, as also are the events which preceded it. It necessarily involves the study of the Jewish soul, its nature, its attitude, its legal processes and its political activities. It must be understood that they have continued to identify themselves with a world revolution, and with strategies for the destruction of Christianity, with the same intensity, and the same avid desire for its crushing, as they demonstrated in the days of Christ's ministry.

Before we move into the panorama of these events, and on through the patterns of the Scriptures, there are certain things we must know about Palestine in the time of Christ.

During the ministry of the man Christ Jesus, the embodiment of God, Messiah, the King, was moving among His people, speaking, proclaiming, opening the eyes of the blind, unstopping the ears of the deaf; performing miracles--so that, even Rome, in its casual first approach to His ministry, testified too, by their procurator in the city of Jerusalem and by the many envoys they sent over to investigate these matters in the land of Palestine.

The fact remains that what remained a mystery, even to Rome, was the hatred and the animosity of official Jewry in Palestine, against a man, who, by their records and all that they had been able to glean as they searched the land of Palestine, had been to do good to those who needed

1

His healing hand, and to speak words that would give spiritual life and hope to a people. In all this--Rome's verdict was: "We see no reason why there is such animosity against this individual."

But in the land of Palestine, these things you must know. Palestine was under the conquest of Rome--a Roman province. The continual administration of Rome over this province was constant from the first hour of its conquest, to the days when the disintegration of the province took place under Titus, the Roman.

It is also to be known that the province of Palestine operated under what was called a theocracy. It was the general policy of Rome to grant a freedom of internal administration to the provinces if they had such a form of government.

The land of Palestine had had a re-entrance by the true tribes of Judah and Benjamin. They wanted to rebuild the city of Jerusalem. This had taken place, as you know, earlier, when in the days of Medo-Persia they left Babylon, returning to their homeland, and rebuilding the Temple and the city of Jerusalem proper.

With them came a mixed multitude of unassimilable people that had no part nor lot with the House of Judah and Benjamin; the same evil power that dominated ancient Babylon, and had moved to Pergamos to establish their headquarters and control.

Here it was that Jesus talked to the Church of Pergamos through the lips and vision of John, when He says of Pergamos, in Revelation, "This is where Satan's seat is." It was here that the House of Herod and other powers extended their authority and manipulated their powers through the money control over Rome, itself; and had

2

bought and gained control of the kingship of the province under the Roman governor, and thus, Herod, King of the Jews, had become ruler over Palestine, and was on the throne at the time of the birth of Christ.

The House of Herod was to retain administration until after the death of Herod the Second; the Tetrarch, as he was known, retained administration at the time of the trial of Jesus Christ. It is a rather significant thing that the Temple at Jerusalem was controlled by a high priesthood. It must be understood that in the days of Moses, Israel was ruled by a supreme court which was made up of 71 personages. This supreme court, even in the time of the kingdom, which existed at the time of Saul and David, and of Solomon, was the real authority for the prosecution and for the hearing of any cases that were capital offenses or even lesser offenses under the various areas of this administration.

Now, this was not a Jewish court. This was a court of your race, operated with the highest standard of jurisprudence, which functioned both in civil and spiritual law, and was recognized by the kingdom as the highest administration. Appeals could always be carried through the priesthood to this court in any matter.

Then, after the dispersion of the ten tribes of Israel in captivity, and Judah and Benjamin into their captivity in the days of Nebuchadnezzar, this court did not operate until Judah and Benjamin returned to rebuild the city of Jerusalem.

Then, this evil, mixed multitude, out of the land of the Herodians, and Pergamos, and those who attached themselves to returning groups of Judah and Benjamin, associated themselves with the rebuilding of the city of Jerusalem. Thus, during that time, there was a division among the people. The Hebrew population of Palestine was divided among the people who made up Judah and Benjamin. If we were to identify these people today, in their second migrations, we would call them the "Normans" and the Germanic people whose coming into Europe was timed exactly with their exodus before the fall of Jerusalem in 70 A.D.

It is important, that when we refer to these people, we note that Judah and Benjamin had a historic background. They had the faith, the religion that had been given them in the days of Moses.

The Pharisees believed in many deep truths. They believed in the resurrection; they believed in the laws of God; they believed in what was known as the written law, and they believed in what was known as the oral law. The writings of the prophets, such as Jeremiah, Isaiah, and others, were added to the knowledge of the law and these, together with spiritual covenants and promises, provided the basis for decisions and action as well as for their hopes and expectations. Thus it was that the advice of the ecclesiastical leaders, which made up the oral law, was called at one time, the Mishnah law, which is under misuse today.

The Pharisees believed in the resurrection. This was not discussed much by Moses at the time of his writings, but was discussed by Job, who preceded him, and by the other prophets who had faith in its expectation!

Besides being "resurrectionists," the Pharisees also believed in and taught the laws of God; the hope of God; the eventual kingdom; the sover-

4

eignty of the white race; and the ultimate things that God was going to develop through it. The development of the two kingdoms in the time of Jeroboam, and their spread through captivity, and the resettling of the ten tribes of Israel in western Europe had not brought the Pharisees of Judah and Benjamin close to the portion of the kingdom that had long since departed in the days of Solomon's son, Rehoboam. But their destiny was to be reunited in a later day.

Now there was another group of people present in Palestine called the Sadducees. Who were they? The Sadducees were made up of Hittites, Canaanites, Amalekites, Herodians, Hashdiums; and these people were not the descendants of Abraham, at all, but they called themselves Jews, and the peoples who lived in the land under their proclamation, were called Jews, although the word "Jew" originally came from the word "Yehudhim," which meant accursed. The fact remains that these people, being Sadducees, had come out of a background of pagan philosophies which had affected India and other parts of the earth; had helped to build and dominate these religions, and were ardent reincarnationists. They operated with a concept that it made no difference what transpired, they would return to get the wealth they had accumulated, the power they had gained, and that they would even expend their lives for this conquest of power. They had no spiritual, ethical, or moral obligation to anything but their creed of obtaining power. They formed a part of the Luciferian descendancy. They were not descendants of Abraham, although they had called themselves Jews, and had attached themselves to the strange theocracy which existed in Palestine at that time.

It was their desire to gain control of this Temple theocracy which had absolute authority under Rome.

So the Sadducees came and demanded seats in the Sanhedrin.

The Sanhedrin, originally, in the background of your race, had 71 judges upon it, and these men were not only supposed to be experts upon theology, and experts on the law as given by God as a mandate to your race in moral, ethical, and sociological problems in spiritual application, but they must be men of high repute; they must have been selected by the people for their high standing in the community in the various provinces of that land, and at that time were elevated to this court by general selection.

From the time that the Sanhedrin was established, it had been perpetuated by replacement with men selected by the Sanhedrin to continue the administration of the standards of divine law.

Under the great Sanhedrin was a lesser Sanhedrin, composed of 23 men. This court could hear cases involving possible capital punishment for crimes of violence resulting in death. This court could not however, sit upon a theological crime that related to blasphemy. Then, there was a third court, composed of three men, which sat only upon lesser grievances. This was called the lesser court. They sat on cases involving such things as petty theft. All these together comprised the complete Sanhedrin.

Throughout the course of history, this had been the process of law. Rome had permitted the administration of Palestine to remain at the Temple level, so the Sanhedrin made up the high court of the land. Hence, the Herodians, those false non-Israelites, whom Jesus was to identify as children of the devil, demanded that they have a share of the seats of the Sanhedrin, according to their number.

Now, under Israelitish law, if it had not been for the conquest by Rome, they would have deported these people as undesirable, and never have permitted them to have any political power whatsoever within their land. Someday, America too will awaken to the truth and deport out of our country this undesirable, unassimilable people who still continue the same subversion they were practicing in the days of Jesus.

Even when the Sanhedrin was thus composed, however, the Pharisees still were in the majority. The Sadducees lacked sufficient numbers to capture an election. They could not appoint for themselves a high priest. They had though, been planning for some time to attain this power. And so one man of influence, who had many servants and a mighty household, Shamah, a Sadducee of the House of Hashdium, and also a relative of the House of Canaan, desired to gain control of the Temple. He said, "I will do this: I will renounce the Sadducees, and proclaim myself a Pharisee. I will proclaim that I accept the principles of the Pharisees, believe in the resurrection, follow Moses, and that I believe in the great spiritual and moral law as well as the written one. Thus, I will number among the Pharisees, and will raise the number of the Pharisees in the Sanhedrin, and they will then have to select members of my House." It was a typical Jewish trick; to proclaim he was something he was not, to gain political power.

We have a word in our English language that has come down from that day to this; the word is

7

"shame." It comes from the name of the man: Shamah; for there was no higher shame than for a person to declare theologically that which was not true in order to gain power over the House of God, to conquer and reduce it to slavery. Thus the false Sadducees, with Roman prestige were seated in the Sanhedrin, posing as Pharisees, and when the election came in 7 A.D., they elected Annas, a Canaanite, high priest. So the Pharisees lost the election because the false Pharisee Canaanites elected one of their own number as high priest. They increased their number with each succeeding priest, and since previous priests of the upper echelon of the ruling House were members of the great Sanhedrin, by the time of Christ, adding their number, 12 were added to the 71. This brought the members that had voting power in the Sanhedrin to 83 instead of the 71 commanded by Mosaic law. It was these 83 who were present at the trial of Jesus Christ.

I want you to know that in reading of the ministry of Christ, we are confused sometimes in the King James version, which is not an original text, by the design of those who helped with its translation to confuse your faith and your race. We are confused by continual reference to peoples by names which are misleading.

In fact, Pharisees, many times under their criticism, should have been translated "Shamah" or "false Pharisees." We see this from the early Alexandrian text, and also from the Aramaic text. The true Pharisees, with a true outlook, were the theologians of that time. The Temple had not only been taken over, at the time of Christ's early boyhood, but at the time of His ministry was dominated by these Canaanite priests, who had turned

it into a house of merchandise. They were deal-
ing in fraud, even selling the animals for sacrifice.
They exploited the people, changing and short-
changing them. They carried on international
banking designs on the steps of the Temple, and
they were charging usurious rates, then, as now.
During His ministry, the Lord Jesus turned and
said to them: "Ye have made my Father's House
a den of murderers, robbers, and thieves." And
He drove the money-changers out of the Temple.

Still the theology of Israel carried on. There
was one young teacher who was a brilliant master,
named Nicodemus. He taught in a school of thought
which was one of the dividing phases of Israel's
theology. Two outstanding men taught. One was
Gamaliel, the other Nicodemus, who taught the
theological students in the Temple. Gamaliel was
a great and honest man, and taught philosophies
related to the thinking of the people. He taught
that God would reach down to forgive violations
of the law, and that the processes of His Spirit
would bring about repentance, because He was
God.

Nicodemus, also an honest man, belonged to
another school of theology, even among the Pharisees, which taught that the individual would have
to make certain decisions and accept certain principles; otherwise he might be cast out into some
area where it would be impossible to discover
him. To identify them today, we would say that
Nicodemus was a Methodist; and we might say
that Gamaliel was a Calvinist or a Baptist. But
their theology was related to the issues of grace.

Originally, the Apostle Paul was taught by
Gamaliel. When Paul became an ardent Christian, you will note that his doctrines were filled

with grace, reflecting the influence of the teachings of Gamaliel, and add to this the Apocalypse of Paul, which he wrote later from his heavenly experience.

These Masters of Israel saw Jesus daily, coming and going from Jerusalem. They heard the words that He said, and they were in actual fulfillment of prophecies they had heard. At one time they were gathered together to hear Jesus speak. They were doctors of law, scribes, and Pharisees from all over Palestine, of every portion and out of every city; they had come to hear what He would say, and what He would do. This meeting had been planned by the Pharisees, to evaluate the messiahship of Jesus.

It was at that meeting that the roof was taken off the building, and a man was lowered down in front of Christ because the press of the crowd was so great that no more people could even get into the building.

It was here that Jesus turned to the man and said, "Thy sins be forgiven thee. Arise, take up thy bed and walk." And when they saw him arise, take up his bed, and walk, a great challenge arose from the Pharisees. Jesus had said, "Thy sins be forgiven thee," and they did not like that; and He said, "Take up thy bed and walk." They were challenged by the miracle. He turned to them and said, "Now which is easier for me to say, 'Thy sins be forgiven thee,' or 'Take up thy bed and walk?'"

This was the revelation of the Messiah with grace that only Yahweh could demonstrate by the remission of transgression.

True Pharisees sat there that day. They beheld these things; and how the Scriptures foretold how they would behold this miracle. They marveled, and they went each man to his own home, and said, "We have seen great things today."

But with each rising miracle, with each new instance of His power, the animosity of the Jews that controlled the Temple increased. They dominated the Sanhedrin, and they were faced with the fact that now, a Messiah, one which they hoped, in the days of Herod they had captured and killed, when the armies of the Jews marched down to Bethlehem and slaughtered the babies. Now they knew He was alive! Now they knew the people were listening to Him.

What was the attitude of ecclesiastical Jewry? Giving lip service to the laws of Moses, but operating under the pattern of the laws of ancient Babylon!

We are told in the 22nd Chapter of Matthew that the Pharisees (Shamah Pharisees, the false Pharisees, actually Sadducees), took counsel how they would try to entangle Christ in His words. This they would do in order to accuse Him and destroy Him. Read the 15th verse of the 22nd Chapter of Matthew. So they took counsel, how they might entangle Him in His speech.

This was only one phase of the conspiracy.

Jesus understood exactly what they were doing; He knew every thought in their minds.

In the 23rd Chapter of Matthew, He said: "I know who you are; you love the uppermost seats, and rooms at the feasts. You want the chief seats in the synagogue. You love the greetings in the market-places. You love to be called Rabbi! Rabbi! But be ye not called Rabbi, for only one is the Master, which is Christ."

Jesus again speaks to them, saying: "Woe

11

unto you, scribes, Shamah Pharisees (false Pharisees), hypocrites, for ye are not only the devourer of the women's houses, through your usury, but you make a pretense of long prayers, for which ye shall receive the greater damnation. Woe unto you, scribes, Pharisees, hypocrites, ye who encompass the sea and the land to make one proselyte to your faith, and making him two-fold more the child of hell than yourselves. Woe unto you, blind guides, which say, 'Whosoever sweareth by the Temple, it is nothing; but whosoever swears by gold, it is authority.' Ye fools, ye blind, which is greater, the gold or the Temple? Whosoever shall swear by the altar is nothing, but whosoever shall swear by some gift to the priesthood, he is guilty."

Jesus continues to say, "Woe unto you Pharisees, scribes, and false hypocrites, ye pay tithes, and ye exact laws in judgment, and ye leave nothing undone, but ye strain at a gnat and swallow a camel, and your judgment is evil.

"You are like white sepulchers, which indeed appear beautiful outwardly, but within are full of dead men's bones from your own uncleanliness. Even so, ye outwardly appear righteous, but ye are filled with hypocracy and iniquity. Woe unto you, because you built the tombs of the prophets and garnished the sepulchres of the righteous."

And then they answered, and they said, "If we had lived in the days of our fathers, we would not have killed the prophets, we would not have destroyed the messengers of God. We would not have spilled their righteous blood."

Then Jesus said, "You have just borne witness of yourselves, that you are the children of the prophet-killers." This is positive identification that they were Canaanites, Hittites and Amalekites, and were not of the House of Abraham. They had borne witness by their very words. Yes, and we hear the same words, today, from B'nai B'rith, in their publications, "If we had lived in the days of Jesus, we would not have crucified Christ." No? They measure up to the full measure of their fathers, for they would crucify the whole Christian world, with their communist revolution.

I turn now to the words of Jesus. He said, "Therefore, you bear witness against yourselves, that you are the children of those that killed the prophets. Fill ye, therefore, the measure of your fathers; this you will do. You are the serpents, you are the generation of the viper. How can you escape the judgment? Behold, prophets, wise men, and scribes ye have killed, and some ye crucified, some ye scourged, or delivered them up to your synagogues, and persecuted them. On you is the judgment of all the righteous blood that has been slain upon the earth, from the blood of righteous Abel to Zacharias, the son of Barachias, whom you slew between the Temple and the altar. Verily, I say all these things in judgment come on this generation. You are the progeny and descendants of Cain, the murderer of Abel, and guilty of every massacre and every assassination of that which is right from that day to this one."

They had attempted to challenge Jesus, the omniscient, incarnate Messiah, who knew every one of them for what they were, and He identified the Jews who controlled the Temple in Jerusalem as Canaanites, and not Israelites, the enemies of the kingdom who had stolen this power.

Let us note the nature of these people in the face of the miracles and the continued doing of

13

good which Christ was performing, for there is no process that is more clear than this situation.

We read these words in the 26th Chapter of Matthew: And it came to pass that when Jesus had finished all these sayings, He said, "You know that after two days from the Feast of the Passover, the Son of Man will be betrayed, and crucified."

We read here that the chief priest and the scribes, the elders of the people, were at the palace of the high priest, called Caiaphas. They consulted how they might take Jesus by subtility, and kill Him.

Hear these words now: Not a process of just law; not a process of jurisprudence, but a conspiracy in the high priest's house. Jesus, not yet having had a trial; these people who were going to preside over His trial had plotted how they might take Him by subtility, and how they might kill Him.

Now, I want to call to your attention these words from the 26th Chapter of Matthew, the 1st to 4th verses: "For they wanted to entrap Him in His talk; they wanted to take Him by subtility, and they had designed to kill Him."

Moreover, they had hired a rascal of their own kind, and had him attach himself to Christ, so that Christ's disciples, who were Galileans and true men of Judah, were always accompanied by one who followed everywhere, offering his services at every opportunity. Jesus knew who he was, that he was a man who would take part in destiny, and He let this man become one of the twelve. Judas immediately demonstrated his affinity: "Oh, I want to carry the money bag." Always his hand was on or in the money sack. He worried about everything that cost a little money, if he didn't control it. Even when a gift of precious

14

ointment was poured over Christ, he said, "How much did it cost, and why isn't it in my sack?"

Jesus was well aware that this fellow was dipping in the bag, and He knew also that he was running to the Temple and getting together with the ADL of that day, and telling them all that Jesus and the disciples were doing.

You say, "How do you know this?" Turn now to the 6th Chapter of the Gospel of John. Here in the closing verses, Jesus makes an identification which is of great importance. He declares to the disciples: "Now, I think you should know, for I have chosen you twelve, and one of you is a devil." People ask me if it was true there was only one Jew among Jesus' disciples? That is correct, only one of them. Jesus said: "I have chosen you twelve, and one of you is a devil."

The 71st verse of the 6th Chapter of John: "And after these things, (after Jesus identified the Ogpu agent) Jesus walked in Galilee, because the Jews sought to kill Him." And it tells us in the 7th Chapter, "When Jesus went down into Galilee, He went down among His brethren, His family, and His friends."

There were no Jews in Galilee; Galilee was where the patriots were, the zealots came from there. Galilee knew what was going on. Even Rome knew that down in Galilee was the resistance. You will find in the record that, angered by the patriots in Galilee, even Pilate sacrificed an occasional Galilean upon the altars, with the sacrifice in Jerusalem. Galilee was the source of the resistance, but the resistance was not Jewish! Galilee was the one place where Jesus had security from the observation of the enemy.

15

When Jesus returned to Jerusalem, at the time of the Feast, Lazarus, Jesus' friend, had just died. After six days, Jesus came to Bethany, where Lazarus was, and raised him from the dead. He called Lazarus out, and the miracle was recorded by Rome. All the land of Palestine began to buzz with it. The Jewish agents standing by were amazed when they saw the raising of Lazarus, and scampered back to the high priest. They counseled among themselves, "When this gets over the land, He's going to take over." And they plotted, it tells us in Sceipture, how to put Lazarus to death again.

Can you imagine anyone, so utterly vile and evil in their thinking, that after a miracle of God raising a man from the dead, their hatred against this miracle was so great that they wished to kill the man all over again?

This gives you a glimpse of the soul of your enemy!

Note now the record of John, the 7th Chapter, we read: "The Pharisees and the people murmured concerning the things which Christ said, and the miracles which He had wrought, so the chief priests and the false Pharisees ordered officers of their army to take Him." Under Roman law, they were permitted an army which could number as many as 3,000 men. At this time there were about 1,600 enlisted in the army, which was controlled by the Temple, and chiefly under the command of certain scribes, or officers of law. It is known that the Roman Palestinian army under the procurator, who was at that time Pontius Pilate, mustered about 7,000 men in the garrisons of Rome. However, we note that the false Pharisees and chief priest sent out officers to take Jesus.

16

When Jesus saw them, He said, "Yet a little while I am here, and then I go to the heavenly Spirits that hold together the heavens and the earth; I go to the plane of the Spirit. Ye shall seek Me (He said to the Jews), but you will not find Me; for where I go, you cannot come."

You will find no Jews in Heaven. People ask if that is true. Well, Jesus said, "You will search for Me, but where I go you cannot come."

Then said the Jews, "Where can He go in the earth, or where shall He go that we shall not find Him?" They had great faith in their ADL in those days. They said, "There's no place He can go that we won't find Him." Why, their Ogpu was everywhere. Then they remembered that the tribes of Israel were in Ephraim, in Britain, and in western Europe, and they wondered, "Just where would He go? Do you suppose He will go out among the ethnos of the nations and to the dispersed among the nations, and teach them?" The dispersed were those of the twelve tribes who had settled in Europe. That was one place they knew they couldn't go, for in Anglo-Saxondom, and in the heart of Germany, it was not permitted for a Jew to enter.

They not only admit this then, but as Jesus continues to speak, the soldiers sent out to seize Him, suddenly in fear, return to the Temple. I quote John, the 8th Chapter, "And the Pharisees and chief officers (Shamah Pharisees) said, 'There never was a man that spoke like this man. He paralyzed us when He spoke. We were afraid to touch Him. The people were spellbound by His words. They were on His side.'" The 'right wing' was waking up, and it wouldn't be safe to take Him away from them.

17

Then the rulers said, "Have any of the prominent Pharisees believed on Him?" And the soldiers answered, "No. It is the people that believe in Him, but they are just masses, cursed already, to be ruled by us forever, so don't worry about them." Nicodemus, who had the right to sit in the Sanhedrin, as a member and a teacher, was present that day because he taught on the steps of the Temple; and when they had these impromptu sessions, he could slip in with them. He said, "Now, just a moment; does our law condemn any man before it hears him?"

They turned and said, "Are you also a Galilean? You are not a Jew, then. Search and see what prophet cometh out of Galilee. He (Jesus) is not a Jew; and you are not one either."

It was this same Nicodemus who came to Jesus by night, of whom they said, "You also are a Galilean, and they went, every man, unto his own house.

This satanic conspiracy had planned to take Jesus and hold Him prisoner, and try Him, before the crowds of people arrived for the Passover. Therefore, when they realized that Christ would not submit to them, and that His miracles were greater than they could contend with, they plotted with subtility how to put Him to death. The 26th Chapter of Matthew tells how Judas Iscariot went to the high priest when they summoned him, and said, "I will betray Him into your hands. I'll tell you where He is going, and I'll identify Him, but what will you pay me for this?" "Oh," said the ADL, "we'll give you thirty pieces of silver." And that is the account of how the Jews bought and sold Jesus, the Master Creator of the Universe, for thirty pieces of silver!

18

They are making much more than that today, for now they are selling America.

I read from the record of the Book of John that Jesus stood in Solomon's porch, preaching openly among the people. The Jews came forth to challenge Him, hoping to trap Him into making a statement which they could charge was blasphemous. For Jesus had identified them in a previous discussion, and they were much disturbed, because Jesus had said, "Ye neither know Me nor my Father. If ye knew Me, you would know the Father, for I and my Father are one. I am going my way. Ye shall seek Me. But every one of you will die in your sins; and where I go, ye cannot come."

Again the Jews questioned among themselves, "Would He kill Himself? Where would He go; where, that we could not find Him?"

Then Jesus said, "I am from above and you are from beneath. I am from out of this world, but you are from under this earth. Therefore, ye shall die in your sins."

And they did not know nor understand that when Jesus said, "He who hath seen Me hath seen the Father, they wist not that He spake to them of the Father."

We return now to the porch of Solomon's Temple. Jesus, in one of His closing addresses here, was surrounded by the Jews. They asked, "Why don't you proclaim whether or not you are the Messiah?"

Jesus said, "I told you, but you believed not. That which I do is in the name and in the nature of my embodied ministry. Therefore I call my sheep by name; I give them eternal life, and they shall never perish. But ye believe not because

19

ye are not of my sheep."

This is a vital testimony: After Jesus had proclaimed to the crowd, "I am not come but to the lost sheep of the House of Israel, " He stated plainly that the Jews were not His sheep. That record you have in the 10th Chapter of John, in these words of the 26th verse.

Now, let us go back over these last moments of Christ's life. He goes with His disciples out into the garden to pray. Jesus was in meditation and prayer. His disciples were sleeping, and Judas Iscariot was with the Temple priests. He had just gotten his thirty pieces of silver, and he was leading their armies and their lesser priests to capture Jesus.

There is something illegal about this that you should know. In the first place, the Sanhedrin does not have authority to sit on a capital crime unless they first gain permission from the procurator of Jerusalem. This would have been Pontius Pilate, whom they did not approach because they wanted to capture, sentence, and slay Him, before the multitudes arrived for the Passover, from Europe, and other distant lands. They were afraid, as we described to you, of the people who wanted to crown Christ king, whose numbers would swell during the Passover, overthrow their evil power, and establish His kingdom; so they said: "We must kill Him now!"

I read this from the 18th Chapter of John: "Judas, then, having received a band of men and officers from the chief priests and Pharisees, came hither now with lanterns, torches, and weapons. And Jesus, knowing all things that should come upon Him, as they went forth, said: "Whom seek ye?"

And they said, "We seek Jesus of Nazareth." Jesus replied, "I am He."

And Judas also, which betrayed Him, stood with them, and he ran over and kissed Jesus on the cheek. This is one of the most obnoxious acts that can be committed by Jewry. They still carry this act on in the supposed brotherhood of Christians and Jews, seeking to woo you into a position of non-resistance to their nefarious schemes for the mastery of the earth.

Jesus turned and looked with scorn, at Judas Iscariot, and said, "Betrayest thou the Son of Man with a kiss!"

The band, the captain, and the officers, took Jesus and bound Him. And they led Him away, first to Annas, who was the father-in-law of Caiaphas, having been upon the throne until the former procurator, six years before, had dis-enthroned Annas, and put his son-in-law Caiaphas upon the throne. Now this was because there had been a fraud involved, and considerable crookedness and graft in the court; which all is on record in Rome today, and I also have the record in my files.

Encircling the court were some palaces and court yards. The Sanhedrin court, which was formerly presided over by Annas, the high priest, still met within his house, though ruled by Caiaphas, his son-in-law.

The Roman governor was Pontius Pilate. Who was Pontius Pilate?

There are some very interesting things you should know about him. He was a Basque, born in Spain, of a rather high family, and had been sent to Britain to be educated in the Druid universities. Being a white man, and of the tribe of Simeon (whether he knew this or not), and having

21

been educated in the universities of London; having traveled through all the chairs of mystery, he belonged to the Masonos; and as he was married to Caesar's daughter, Claudia, he was the son-in-law of the emperor of Rome. It was because of this that he had received his appointment as governor of Jerusalem. So Pontius Pilate, governor of Jerusalem, was an Israelite. He was a white man, of the same racial background as all members of the Anglo-Saxon, Scandinavian, Nordic, Germanic, Basque, and Lombardic people. He was a brilliant, well educated man, and he knew the words and symbols of mystery, but he was not aware of the great spiritual things which time was to unveil, and experiences which were later to be his and which he would, in part, record.

So now he was governor of Jerusalem. He had experienced many troubles since he had been there because of the constant blackmailing attempts of the money masters, from the Isle of Pergamos and Jerusalem, to control the Roman Empire.

Now, I want to point out to you that as Jesus was being led bound, through the streets, he was being taken to the house of Annas. A young theological student saw them on the street, with Jesus a prisoner. This man's name was John Barnabas. Later, he became one of the disciples that traveled with the Apostle Paul. Now, John Barnabas was a student of Gamaliel. He was daily at the steps of the Temple, and this honest and upright teacher had trained him in the standards of Israel, and in the principles of law.

He was also a friend of Nicodemus, and enjoyed going to the house of Nicodemus and disputing with him over differences in theology.

He saw that these soldiers were forcibly taking Christ, whom they all now respected as a great teacher, and considered to be the Messiah. For after Nicodemus had talked with Jesus by night, he came back to say, "This man is Messiah."

He saw that they had taken Christ prisoner, and were going to the house of Annas, the high priest. So he ran to Nicodemus saying, "I just saw them with Jesus, in bonds; they are leading Him to the house of Annas, the high priest."

Nicodemus knew they had recently captured Barabbas, the patriot and nationalist, and the leader of those who hoped someday to protect the Messiah. So the captivity of Christ was a dangerous thing.

Nicodemus said, "John Barnabas, hasten now to the house of Gamaliel and tell him: 'Though I sit in the Sanhedrin, I have not been notified.'" Then he asked, "Did you note who were gathering?"

"Yes," said Barnabas, "the Sadducees were gathering at the house of Annas."

Nicodemus said, "This is therefore, an illegal Sanhedrin. The Sanhedrin cannot sit at night."

In my library, I have the records of many years of Sanhedrin gatherings, and it was clearly illegal for a Sanhedrin to meet at night, as it was illegal for them to make an arrest at night, unless someone was in flight. It takes many days for such a trial to be consummated. The prisoner was to be taken one day, and to hear his accusers the second day. He had the right to gather his own witnesses the third day, and make his presentation on the fourth day. An evaluation was made on the fifth day, and sentence was passed on the sixth day. If there was to be an execution, it could not take place on the Sabbath, and therefore must be carried over to the eighth day. If the Sanhedrin had met in the middle of the week, and they started the court on a Thursday, it had to be carried over as we have declared.

Nicodemus walked in and found Jesus in the house of Annas, the high priest, surrounded by a group of Sadducees, Canaanite Jews.

The Gospel of John contains this account: "And Jesus was brought bound into the presence of this high priest. And when He was brought into the presence of Annas, the high priest, they asked Jesus this question, 'What is your doctrine?' And Jesus answered, 'I spoke openly in the Temple and before the synagogue. Now I don't have to bear witness against myself to please you. I know the law. Now, if you want to know what I said, why don't you ask the people who heard me? If you have charges against me, bring in your witnesses.'"

The high priest was angry at Christ's answers.

Jesus added: "I ever talked before the people openly. It was not in secret. Why askest thou me these things?" And one of Annas' Jew officers reached out and slapped Jesus across the face. This was another violation of the law. They could not even, legally, touch a man until his conviction.

Jesus said, "If I have spoken evil, bear witness of Me. By what right has thou smitten me, as I have done no evil?"

It was at that moment that Nicodemus had moved into the house of Annas and sat down. The scribe saluted and said, "The Rabbi Nicodemus takes his seat in the Sanhedrin."

24

Then Nicodemus said, "The Sanhedrin cannot sit at night. I do not take a seat in the Sanhedrin. The Sanhedrin is not under the auspices of the high priest, and this cannot be a Sanhedrin."

They then said to the scribe, "How readest thou?"

The scribe said, "I must concur with the Rabbi Nicodemus."

From this moment we witness an acceleration of the plot against the Master.

Now we turn to the 26th Chapter of the Book of Matthew: And they laid hold then upon Jesus, and led Him away to Caiaphas, the high priest, where the scribes and the elders were assembled.

Nicodemus looked about. They had not notified one Pharisee; because by now, most of the Pharisees were on the side of Jesus. They believed in the resurrection, and they recognized Him as the miracle prophet. They saw the things which had happened from the resurrection of Lazarus, and they were convinced that this was the Messiah.

So the scribes couldn't get a quorum of Pharisees to sit with them, and they didn't want to notify them because their votes might upset the situation. The Pharisees could alarm the people, and great catastrophe would fall upon these Jews, called Sadducees, who held this priesthood by the process of fraud, as Jesus identified.

When they came in to sit down, they sat, every Sadducee, and in stalked Nicodemus, from the house of Annas, and they said: "The Rabbi Nicodemus takes his seat in the great Sanhedrin." Nicodemus: "This is not a Sanhedrin. The Sanhedrin cannot sit at night." They said to the scribe: "How readest thou?" Said the scribe: "I have to concur with the Rabbi Nicodemus." Then they said: "This council shall proceed, and hear the charges. Every man be seated."

Which to this day is the way the Jews carry out most of their processes of jurisprudence. This was quickly followed by the entrance of Gamaliel. Angrily he asked: "What goes on here?"

They replied, "Silence! Request thy answer only from the high priest." The high priest said: "The great Sanhedrin sits upon a malefactor, and a blasphemer."

Gamaliel replied, "Does any court judge a man before it hears his case? How can the Sanhedrin sit at night? How hast thou seized this man at night? How canst thou bring Him to trial? How can this thing happen in the land of Israel?"

It is recorded that the chief priests and the elders that had assembled at the house of Caiaphas and as the Sanhedrin, then held a brief recess to seek false witnesses against Jesus, in order to put Him to death. Matthew, 26: 59.

They sent out for false witnesses! Nice people, these Jews. You may think that this is only in the King James version. No. I have a record from the Sanhedrin to the effect that they sent out for false witnesses. We read a little further: "And they found none, even among the false witnesses, who had character enough to stand up and be able to give their prosecution." In other words, every false witness they sent out to buy was such a rascal, he couldn't stand up in court anyhow, because everyone knew they were paid perjurers. Finally, they found two witnesses that were acceptable by their standards, who came to their illegal court and said, "This man said: 'I will destroy the Temple of God, and I will build it in three days." The high priest arose and said: "Answerest Thou nothing? What is it that these witnesses say against Thee? What has Thou to say?"

Jesus had already said to Caiaphas: "If I tell you the truth you won't believe Me, so why should I bother to answer you?" Jesus had already said: "Ye cannot understand my words, because you cannot hear my speech. You have no spiritual capacity to hear this, being from beneath, having no communion with that which is from above."

So as Jesus held his peace, the high priest said, "I adjure Thee by the living Yahweh that Thou tellest whether Thou be Yahshua, the embodied Messiah." Now this was the one question they wanted Him to answer, so they could then judge Him.

Jesus said, "Thou hast already said it. Nevertheless, this will I tell ye: Even you shall see the Son of Man seated in authority and power in the heavens and you are going to behold Him coming with power and glory from the clouds of the heavens." And the high priest rent his clothes. So this false priest, who had no interest in righteousness anyhow, a complete rascal, charges that Jesus is guilty of blasphemy, and says: "What need have we of any further witnesses? We accuse this man of blasphemy."

Nicodemus and Gamaliel rose to their feet. They said, "Thou hast not established that this man is not the Messiah. Thou hast not established that what He said is blasphemy. He said to you, 'Thou shalt behold the embodiment of God coming out of the heavens with great power.' Now, therefore, how canst thou judge Him?"

But the high priest ignored Nicodemus and

Gamaliel, and said, "What think you?" And the cry of the Jews, the Sadducees, went up from this evil-filled Sanhedrin: "He is guilty! Crucify Him!" You can read it right here in the Gospel of Matthew.

Then they spit upon Him. They buffeted Him. They struck Him with the palms of their hands, and said: "Now, prophecy unto us Christ, Messiah. Prophecy, who hit you that time?" And they punched Him from behind, and they punched Him from the side, and they struck Him again. They said, "Now from behind your back, who hit you?" And Gamaliel and Nicodemus walked out of that Sanhedrin to call for the Pharisees, and the followers of Barabbas, to throw all Jerusalem into uproar, and to rescue Christ, if they could.

The Jews had sentenced Christ illegally, but they knew they dared not, themselves, execute the judgment. What were they to do? In the 15th Chapter of Matthew we read that as it was approaching the morning, two o'clock, to be exact, for the dawn had not yet come. The chief priests, consulting with their elders and scribes in the council, took Jesus bound, and hurriedly delivered Him to Pilate. They awoke Pilate from his sleep; called him to come down to the judgment hall.

Pilate said, "Why should I come to the judgment hall? Why do you disturb me from my sleep?"

They said: "If you are a friend of Caesar's, you will come down. This is a grievous matter, and we demand that you come at once."

Now normally, nobody could get a governor out of his bed at such an hour to hear a case. Certainly not at two o'clock in the morning, but

28

people should know by now that there is a lot of action when Jews snap their fingers. Many people today, just as in the days of Jesus, are afraid to speak openly, even as you may read in the 7th Chapter of the Book of John, "The peoples of Galilee and Jerusalem were afraid to speak openly for fear of the Jews." So it was in this instance, they acted, for fear of the Jews.

And now, in the record we read that Pilate had Christ brought into his presence, and ushered Him into the judgment hall. Pilate turned to Jesus, and asked Him, "Art Thou the king of the Judeans?"

Jesus said, "Thou sayest it."

Then Pilate turned to the chief priests, who accused Jesus of many things in their own court. They said he was a blasphemer; as a man, he maketh Himself God. But now, standing before Pilate, they said, "He would make Himself a king in place of Caesar." Now the charge is no longer blasphemy, but sedition.

How fantastically wicked are the ways of these people who poke their way into our nation, hate our Christianity, and then, if anybody exposes them, they charge them with sedition. It has even happened here, in our own country.

Come with me now into the Book of Matthew, where we shall hear what transpires in Pilate's judgment hall. I think it is more important that you hear and remember this, as it relates to the trial of Christ, than almost any passages that have been recorded. For now, they had delivered Jesus unto Pontius Pilate, and whereas until now the attempt to destroy Jesus had been carried on a charge of blasphemy, now, before Pontius Pilate, since they were anxious to destroy Him at once,

29

the charge was changed before Pilate, to read that He was an enemy of Caesar. So, they, with their torches and lanterns, had awakened the governor, and Jesus stood before Pontius Pilate; and Pilate, as he turned to the accusers, said, "What accusation bring you against this man?"

They said: "If He were not a malefactor and a criminal, we wouldn't bring Him to you." Pilate replied, "Well then, if He is a malefactor, why don't you judge Him under your law?" They said: "Because we want to kill Him, and we are not permitted to kill Him under the Roman arrangement. You have to kill Him." Pontius Pilate: "Oh, is that so?" He then again entered into the judgment hall, called Jesus and asked, "Art Thou the king of the Judeans?"

Jesus said, "Thou hast said it. (Did someone tell this to you or did you think this out for yourself?)" Then Pilate answered Him and said, "Am I a Jew? These people, supposedly Thy nation, deliver Thee unto me. What hast Thou done?" Jesus answered, "My kingdom is not in this era."

Now, this was a true answer. It meant there was no challenge to Caesar at this time of Christ, or of His trying to take over Caesar's government. "My kingdom is not in this era. If my kingdom were of this era, my servants would fight, and I would not be delivered to the Jews."

"My kingdom is hence," Jesus answered him.

"Art Thou therefore, then a king?"

"Thou sayest that I am a king. To this end was I born. For this cause came I into the world, that I should bear witness of the truth." Every Royal Arch Mason knows that this struck a vital chord: "I came to bear witness of the truth."

Something stirred, nostalgically, in the mind of Pilate! He remembered his own training in the Druid schools of London, before he married Caesar's daughter. He now knew there was something strange in this matter, and he turned to Jesus and answered Him with the proper answer, "What is truth?"

And Jesus returned him the answer, which is not recorded at this time in the Gospel according to St. John. Some of you know why it is not there. But He answered Pilate, and the moment He answered, Pilate knew that here was a Masonos, a Master Mason, a son of the Most High, and he knew that he was duty bound to do here the thing which was right

Pilate then went out unto the Jews, and said, "I have interrogated this man." Now this is the supreme judge located in Palestine. "I have interrogated this man. I have heard your charges. I pronounce Him NOT GUILTY. I find no fault in this man."

And then the cry goes up: "Don't you know that this man is a revolutionist, a seditionist, a zealot? He stirs up all Galilee!"

Pontius Pilate turned and said, "Is this man a Galilean?"

They said, "Surely He is a Galilean. He is not a Jew."

Remember this now! This is part of Roman record: "Surely He is a Galilean. HE IS NOT A JEW."

Then said Pilate, "The king in Jerusalem under me is Herod. So, therefore, I'll send Him down to Herod. He is in Herod's jurisdiction." So, he then sent Jesus down to Herod.

We are told that Herod had long been anxious

31

to meet Jesus, because he had heard of the miracles He had performed. So when He entered the court, Herod said, "Why don't you do a few miracles? Do a few tricks for me. Show me what you can do." Jesus would not answer Herod. This evil Jew wasn't worthy of an answer. Jesus looked at him with disdain. Here was one of Lucifer's sons. He looked like some of the hock shop proprietors in your society today, and Jesus wouldn't answer him. He didn't owe this fellow an answer. So, Herod brought forth a robe of purple and put it on Jesus. They scourged Him and put a crown of thorns on His head. Then they sent Him back to Pilate. Pilate said to Jesus, "I wouldn't dare make a judgment in Thy mighty and august presence. Thou art greater than I am. We will let this be settled by you."

In the meantime, warned in a dream, the wife of Pontius Pilate, herself secretly a disciple, came to see her husband and said, "Don't you judge Him. For I not only know of Him, but I have been warned in a vision that this man, over whom you are standing in judgment, is incarnate God."

Pilate was very much shaken. They brought Jesus before him, and the soldiers, returning with His robe, said, "Hail, king of the Jews!" and were smiting Him. Then Pilate came forth, said, "Behold, I now bring forth unto you a man that ye may know, and again I find no fault in Him."

This was the second time the judge had said, "This man is not guilty." Have you ever heard of a case like this, where they could put pressure on the judge, and hear the whole case over again in a few minutes?

Five hours go by. Then Pilate said, "Behold the man!" The chief priests cried, "Crucify Him!" Pilate asked them, "Why don't you take Him and crucify Him? For the third time, I find no fault in him." Read the 19th Chapter of the Gospel according to St. John.

The Jews answered, "We have a law, and by our law, He is to die because He revealed Himself as the embodiment of God."

Pilate said, "That is your theology. I am not interested in your theology. He has not violated any of the laws of Rome. I'm going to let Him go."

They said, "If you let Him go, you are no friend of Caesar. He would gather up all the people and overthrow Rome."

Jesus answered not a word.

Pilate spoke to Jesus, "Don't you know I could crucify Thee, and I also have the power to release Thee?"

And Jesus answered Pilate: "You have no power, except I give it thee." This frightened Pilate even more.

So, seeking a way out, Pilate said to the people, "We have a custom of Roman leniency in the provinces where we rule; it is a custom, once a year, to let someone out of prison. Now we have a man in prison, Barabbas, the captain of the secret armies that have stolen from your caravans, and fought you; who even fights Rome, and has been charged with crimes of murder, because in the battle he killed Roman soldiers. Now who would you rather have me turn loose on you, the captain of this nationalist army of outlaws, the leader of the secret army, or Jesus, who has healed your sick and spoken in your presence?"

A steady stream of witnesses then came, stood before Pilate, and testified concerning the miracles that Jesus did, and the good that he performed.

All this is recorded in the Gospel of Nicodemus, for the scribe also sat in the court of Pontius Pilate and recorded all the conversation. The 5th Chapter of the Gospel of Nicodemus tells you every word that was said during those discussions.

Pilate would have released Him, but they said: "No, give unto us Barabbas, and crucify Christ!"

Pontius Pilate turned to Jesus again, not willing to sentence Jesus to death. Three times he had said: "I find no fault in this man; He is a just man; He has done nothing wrong, all the witnesses bear testimony that He does good."

All this time, Pontius Pilate knew that Jesus was a brother of wisdom and a master of the lodge of his own education. Pilate didn't want to be involved. He was warned by his wife who had a feeling of impending trouble. Now he turned to Jesus and asked, "What shall I do?"

Jesus said to Pontius Pilate: "You are in a spot that is very tight for you, because this is a part of destiny. This was known before the foundation of the world. You have just walked into this spot of destiny. You cannot help yourself, and are not responsible for what is going on. Therefore, I want you to do exactly what is written. I am not going to hold it against you. Do what is written."

Pilate said: "Well, what is written?"

Jesus said: "It is written they shall take me and crucify me."

Pilate said: "I could not be responsible for that decision."

There was a custom in Israel, as well as in Britain, wherever white men stalked the earth: a covenant of water. Pilate said: "Bring me a basin of water." The water was brought to him. He dipped his hands in the water and raised them before the people, saying: "Don't count me a party to your crime. I wash my hands of the responsibility of the blood of this just man."

Now a great many preachers, without knowing the things we have discussed with you tonight, have been castigating Pilate from that day to this. How many sermons have been preached that you can't wash your hands of Jesus? How many times have they denounced Pilate? Pilate had just been told by Jesus: "You do what is written." Jesus told him what was written, and what he would have to do, in performing his place in history.

So, Pontius Pilate had said: "All right, I'll follow that instruction. I'll do what is written, but I'm not going to have the responsibility on my hands." And he washed his hands of that responsibility. This was a legal act. Pontius Pilate would not and did not condemn Christ. He would let the law of the Sanhedrin condemn Him, but assume no responsibility because Jesus had said: "Do it thus."

I want you to remember that the cry came from the Jews as Pilate washed his hands of Jesus. They said, "That's all right with us; His blood be upon our children."

May that rest until God is willing to lift it in the fullness of His own time, because any judgment that has fallen upon them, has not been persecution, but retribution! They have not changed their evil ways.

Remember these things concerning the trial of the Son of God. The Jewish trial was illegal. It met at night. The Jewish trial was sought to be tried with false witnesses. The Jewish trial did not provide Jesus any defense. The Jewish trial would not hear those who stood in His defense. The Jewish trial violated all the laws of Moses, and all the laws of the Sanhedrin. And they smote Him. And they spit upon Him. They never sought for evidence of His identity. The Jewish court sentenced Him to death, but lacked the courage to perform it. Then, turning Him over to Rome, wanted Rome to take the responsibility for His death.

You will note also that Pilate, Masonic in his background, and desirous, because of the vision, to set Christ free, wanted no part in this matter. Though he had had a full coverage of the events of Christ's life from the hour that the challenges were brought to the procurator's home and his palace, but he found no fault in Christ.

In my library, I have the report of Pontius Pilate, to Tiberius Caesar, concerning what happened after His crucifixion. I have the report of his defense when Pilate was called to stand before Julius Caesar, and give an account of the things that had happened under his administration, and during the time of Christ, His crucifixion and His resurrection.

I just want to add this: Pontius Pilate became a converted and complete, accepting follower of Jesus. He was one of the most ardent, staunch admirers of Christ, and after the resurrection, became identified with the early companies of Christians. He stood before Caesar, after his wife had borne her testimony some years later, and told him what had happened, and Caesar asked of Pilate, "Has thy wife become a Christian, and art thou also a Christian?" And Pilate replied, "Yes, I will take my lot with His, and I will stand with Jesus who rose from the dead."

And Pontius Pilate's wife passed away, directly in front of Julius Caesar, and they offered unto Pilate the fatal cup, and he took the cup, a Roman patrician to the last, refusing to give up his faith in Christ. The son-in-law of Caesar died with the testimony of Christ upon his lips!

In your time, the trial of Christ will always remain open, for Jesus was the judge and the victor. "Where I go you cannot come. I am from above, and you are from beneath. You who judge Me have no power. You who judge Me are standing in the presence of the Most High God."

And to His disciples, and those who were to take up the challenge of His Spirit that He poured out upon them, He said, "The hour will come, which is hence, when my servants will fight. The kingdom will not be given to the Jews."

You and I know that the kingdom of God has suffered violence, that the violent take it by storm. We are on the edge of a new day. The great spiritual forces of God stir the forces of right which are within our nation, awakening to challenge the evil influences that dominate our society, and seek to bind us with the Marxist policy of Anti-Christ.

I tell you that in this day, and in this hour, God is raising up the mighty strength of his kingdom, and shall rejoin that kingdom for the greatest hour of victory in the history of the world! And so, we close for the moment, this phase of the trial of Christ.

We have approached it from another set of records which relate to it, and the story of Rome is even more challenging. Even Roman guards before Pilate couldn't hold the standards of Rome when Christ approached! The very standards bent almost double. Two strong men on each stave couldn't keep the Roman standards from bowing before Christ.

This impressed Pilate, and angered the Jews. But before Him, as prophecy had declared, "Every standard shall dip, and all men shall proclaim that He is King of Kings, and Lord of Lords."

During this time of remembering the resurrection, these events surrounding the life of Christ impress all Christendom. It is a part of the visitation of our God to His children. Since the children of God were embodied in bodies of flesh, He took upon Himself the same flesh. He is not ashamed to call you His brethren, the race He established for His kingdom. And the victory is assured.

We have watched many changes sweep the world. We are a great nation and a company of nations. We have great technology and a mighty civilization, but we have not yet learned to know our enemies, and set the armor of God in array against them. But we shall, in this day!

www.ingramcontent.com/pod-product-compliance
Lightning Source LLC
La Vergne TN
LVHW021548080426
835509LV00019B/2916